JAMES THRALL SOBY

BEN SHAHN 379

THE MUSEUM OF MODERN ART, NEW YORK
PENGUIN BOOKS

THE PENGUIN MODERN PAINTERS

Editor: Sir Kenneth Clark

American Editor: Alfred H. Barr, Jr.

Made in Great Britain

Colour plates printed by
John Swain & Son, Ltd., London and Barnet
Text pages printed at
The Baynard Press, London

Published by Penguin Books Limited
West Drayton, Middlesex, England
The Museum of Modern Art
11 West 53 Street, New York 19

1947

BEN SHAHN

"ALL ART," wrote Roger Fry in *Vision and Design*, "gives us an experience freed from the disturbing conditions of actual life." If we accept this definition, then we must reject much of Ben Shahn's painting, as Fry rejected Bruegel's, for it does more than remind us of the living world; it takes strong issue with contemporary reality, and urges us to sympathetic choice. Shahn himself is the opposite of the "pure" painter nourished in his studio by esthetic faith. He prefers to work part of the week for a labor union or a government bureau, leaving the rest of his time for painting. He feels that he needs this contact with social activity, since otherwise, he says with alarm, "I might be left with a paintbrush in my hand."

In general conviction Shahn has not lacked precursors, of course—Daumier in the nineteenth century, George Grosz in our own, to mention two of the greatest. But what is exceptional about him is that he has been able to effect so direct a translation of his easel art into social instrument, as when he converts some of his paintings into posters by the sole addition of lettering. Moreover, the transfer of function works equally well in reverse; *The Welders* (plate 25) was originally designed as a poster, and is among his most impressive paintings. The same interchangeability applies in another connection. He has twice executed pictures for specific advertising purposes. One of these, rejected by the commissioning agency, survives as a poetic easel painting (plate 17).

In a word, Shahn's vision is all of one piece. As propagandist he is involved in mass appeal on the far-flung scale peculiar to our times, and consequently faces an insistent temptation to sacrifice quality for communicability. He never yields. His paintings, posters, murals, advertisements, proceed from the same steady eye and

3

are informed by a relentless integrity. All, *pace* Mr. Fry, are art of uncompromising order.

Like several leading American artists of today, Shahn was born in Russia of Jewish parents and came to this country as a child. His heritage is apparent, not only in the larger matters of his compassion and emotional frankness, but also at times in his stylistic usage. His love of bright, flowered patterns (plate 19) and his persistent response to festive occasion (plates 21, 29) seem related to folk-art traditions. Yet since 1931, when he suddenly reached maturity as an artist, he has been unmistakably an American painter, as American as nineteenth century genre artists like Charles Caleb Ward and Eastman Johnson. On the whole he has not shared the earlier painters' devotion to homely anecdote, though sometimes he has drawn near them in this regard, if always on far less obtrusive terms. The *Four Piece Orchestra* (plate 22), for example, is at least secondarily notable for its humor and for the story-telling contrast of overalled figures to a cellist whose clothes and manner suggest the trained musician.

It is interesting to note how frequently Shahn portrays men informally playing musical instruments, for his art is often so closely identified with American episode that it furnishes a visual parallel to our epic folk songs. Significantly, he remembers himself most clearly as a child listening to a band (plate 21). His pictures of the ordeal of Sacco and Vanzetti (plates 2, 3), his painting of the blind accordionist who played out his grief when Roosevelt's funeral procession passed (plate 1)—are akin in simplicity, fervor and tenacity of refrain to such songs as "John Brown's Body" and the modern anti-lynching ballad, "Southern Trees Bear a Strange Fruit."

But whatever the relation of Shahn's painting to folk art and folk songs, he is in no sense a primitive artist. If some of his pictures belong to a series conceived on Sunday excursions through the New Jersey countryside (plate 12), this is because his subjects are relaxed on that day, and he has always been interested in what people do when in theory they do nothing at all. Far from being a "Sunday painter," Shahn knows everything that can be of use to him about the advanced forms of contemporary art here and abroad. His paintings are far from abstract; indeed, they are nearly all utterly committed to subject. Yet his fine control of

4

placing has benefited from the lessons of cubism and its satellite movements; his work is as inspired in structure as in humanistic content, a fact which once or twice has caused left-wing critics to accuse him of unduly subordinating message to form. It would be difficult, indeed, to think of another living American artist who has so successfully applied abstract precedent to a personal realism. And his line, though it often carries great satirical weight (plates 2, 5), can also have the autonomous, hieroglyphic intensity of Paul Klee's drawing, which Shahn reveres.

When Shahn arrived in this country from his native Kovno in 1906, he was already absorbed in drawing, and as a child growing up in the poor sections of Brooklyn, he was often bullied by local toughs into making sidewalk sketches of their sporting idols, working always under a threatening injunction to be exact. From 1913 to 1917 he attended high school at night and during the day was employed as a lithographer's apprentice. He continued to support himself at lithography until 1930, with interruptions, and perhaps this long training accounts in part for the precision with which he now handles such pictorial details as intricate patterns of fabric or minute lettering; certainly it helps to explain the technical proficiency of his lithographed posters.

Shahn's realism is not, however, merely stylistic. It is a fundamental of his philosophic approach. One of the most imaginative of modern American painters, he ordinarily insists on accuracy in his choice and execution of subsidiary motifs. "There's a difference," he says, "in the way a twelve-dollar coat wrinkles from the way a seventy-five-dollar coat wrinkles, and that has to be right. It's just as important esthetically as the difference in the light of the Ile de France and the Brittany Coast. Maybe it's more important." When he includes automobiles in his compositions, they must be of a make and vintage their owners could afford; if architecture appears, he prefers to have seen its prototype in fact or print. His love of exactitude pertains not only to inanimate accessory but to human contour: the feet and the postures of the boys in *Peter and the Wolf* (plate 17) evoke a sharp memory of American childhood; the springy stance of the youth in the right foreground of *Handball* (plate 15) is unforget-

5

tably real. Shahn consistently uses photographs as points of reassurance, and until recent years himself worked expertly at photography. He is no less inventive than the most orthodox surrealist, but he gravely suspects loose flights of fancy. Like John Hersey, who gives in *Hiroshima* the exact trade names of Japanese sewing machines found in the atomic wreckage, Shahn insists on the facts he transcends.

When he graduated from high school, Shahn attended New York University and then City College of New York, leaving the latter in 1922 to study at the National Academy of Design. In 1925 and again in 1927 he went abroad, and traveled in France, Italy, Spain and North Africa. In Paris he absorbed the art of the living masters, especially, if rather incongruously, Rouault and Dufy. He returned home in 1929, and the following year exhibited at the Downtown Gallery in New York a number of watercolors of African subjects and three studio compositions in oil. There is little in these early works, except quick vigor of line, to indicate the artist he was to become.

In 1930 he went to live at Truro, Cape Cod, and painted a number of small beach scenes in the casual, expressionist technique he had acquired abroad. Then he made up his mind. "I had seen all the right pictures," he says, "and read all the right books—Vollard, Meier-Graefe, David Hume. But still it didn't add up to anything. 'Here am I,' I said to myself, 'Thirty-two years old, the son of a carpenter. I like stories and people. The French school is not for me.'"

He turned first to racial themes, completing twelve remarkable border illustrations for a copy of the Haggada, followed by ten watercolors on the Dreyfus case. "Then I got to thinking about the Sacco-Vanzetti case... Ever since I could remember I'd wished that I'd been lucky enough to be alive at a great time—when something big was going on, like the Crucifixion. And suddenly I realized I was. Here I was living through another crucifixion. Here was something to paint!" Within seven months he had completed twenty-three gouache paintings on the trial of the American-Italian anarchists, Nicola Sacco and Bartolomeo Vanzetti, convicted of the murder, on April 15, 1920, of a paymaster and his guard in South Braintree, Massachusetts.

A detailed summary of the aberrations of

6

the Sacco-Vanzetti trial was published in the *Atlantic Monthly* for March, 1927, by the Honorable Felix Frankfurter, who became legal advisor to the Sacco-Vanzetti Defence Committee. In brief, no reliable evidence had been adduced to prove that the defendants were at the scene of the crime, nor had any of the stolen payroll been traced to them. In the hysterical atmosphere of a "Red" hunt then sweeping the country, the two men were nevertheless convicted of murder in the first degree on July 14, 1921, and the presiding judge, Webster Thayer, denied an appeal for a retrial on the tenuous legal grounds that Sacco and Vanzetti exhibited "consciousness of guilt." His summary of the case was riddled with prejudice, his charge to the jury virtually a plea for conviction. But thanks to the efforts of Labor and fair-minded men of all stations, the case dragged on for six years. An appeal to the State Supreme Court failed. As a last resort, Governor Fuller of Massachusetts was deluged with demands for a pardon. His investigating committee, with President Lowell of Harvard as chairman, issued an unfavorable report, and the defendants were executed in August, 1927.

The patent injustice of the Sacco-Vanzetti case inspired fevered demonstrations in the United States and, indeed, throughout the world. But Shahn's series of paintings is remarkable for its restraint. Its accusation is the more deadly for clinging to fact and avoiding extravagant caricature and allegorical disguise: it threads protest through the needle of reality. *The Lowell Committee* (plate 2), to be sure, is a scalding satirical image, but for the most part the impact of the series comes from its laconic dignity. Judge Thayer, for example, is not presented as a monster, but as a high court functionary, the very man who did what he did, though his narrow eyes and pendulous ear give a clue to inflexibility of mind. Most of the other characters in the case—the defendants, their families, the witnesses, the prosecutors—are depicted much as they appeared in stark press photographs. Yet gradually we become aware how skilful has been the painter's intensification of truth. The handling of the background in *The Lowell Committee* is exceptionally imaginative, and illustrates a recurrent factor in Shahn's art: the use of architectural setting as both psychological foil to human figures and

7

as expressive abstract pattern. The line which moulds the paneling in *Sacco and Vanzetti* (plate 3) goes beyond the descriptive to create a glowing palimpsest. And in the latter picture, for all its understatement, the moral fervor of Vanzetti plays against Sacco's rougher honesty, so that we need no further reminder that it was Vanzetti who spoke the moving valedictory: "Our words—our lives—our pains nothing! The taking of our lives—the lives of a good shoemaker and a poor fish peddler—all! That last moment belongs to us—that agony is our triumph."

Among the visitors to the New York exhibition of the Sacco-Vanzetti pictures was Diego Rivera, then at work on his murals for Rockefeller Center which were later destroyed for political reasons. Impressed by the exhibition, Rivera hired Shahn as an assistant in the spring of 1933; his influence on the younger painter reached its climax in the latter's first completed mural commission at Roosevelt, New Jersey (plate 6). Meanwhile, during the summer and fall of 1932, Shahn had completed a second series of small gouache paintings on a public issue—the case of the persecuted labor leader,

Tom Mooney. The didactic force of the series is no greater than that of the Sacco-Vanzetti panels, but there is an evident advance in technical assurance. The color, mostly muted and solemn the previous year, now became brilliant and light; yellows, pinks and fresh greens replaced the browns and blacks of the Sacco-Vanzetti gouaches. At the same time, the forms grew bolder, the use of contrasting motifs more skilled. In *Two Witnesses* (plate 5) a tremulous line supplies the devastating facial characterization, but the huge yellow hat shows the painter moving in the direction of Lautrec's compositional boldness. The same new freedom is apparent in Shahn's image of the California governor who refused Mooney a pardon (plate 4). The figure's vacuous cordiality is suffocatingly real, yet there is more than iconic power to admire in the picture as a whole. The volumes are freely and eloquently distorted for emotive purposes, the opposition of pink automobile to the governor's yellow waistcoat is as arbitrary—and as sensitive—as the French Symbolists' transmutations of natural color.

In 1933 Shahn was enrolled in the Federal Government's Public Works of Art Project, and presently completed eight small tempera panels on Prohibition, of which the finest is here reproduced (plate 7). His reference to architecture is more detailed in this series than ever before, and he makes frequent use of recessive diagonals as wings to human drama, possibly as a result of his mural training under Rivera. At this period, encouraged by the brilliant American photographer, Walker Evans, Shahn took numerous photographs of New York street scenes, emphasizing an unposed intimacy between figures and setting. He also became interested in America's insistent public typography—its signs, printed slogans, posters, advertisements—and in the Prohibition series he uses this typography as a choral accompaniment to his figures' actions, while in later paintings its function becomes more purely atmospheric. There results a strangely appealing inner commentary, text within pictorial illustration. Similarly, Shahn often suggests by title and subject a music we cannot hear (plate 13).

From September, 1935 to May, 1938, Shahn worked for the Farm Security Administration as an artist and, very briefly, as a photographer, with the euphemistic title of "Senior Liaison Officer" to guarantee him a living wage. But he had previously undergone the most bitter experience of his thorny early career. In 1934 he and a fellow-artist, Lou Block, had been commissioned by the Federal Emergency Relief Administration to prepare murals for the penitentiary at Riker's Island in New York Harbor. The commission involved months of research and a detailed first-hand documentation of prison conditions; its iconographic plan was to show on opposite walls of a main prison corridor the contrasting aspects of old and reformed penal methods. The completed sketches, almost entirely Shahn's work, were approved by the Mayor and the Commissioner of Correction, but were rejected by the academic-minded Municipal Art Commission in 1935 as "artistically, and in other respects . . . unsatisfactory and unsuitable for the location for which they were intended." A poll of prisoners at another jail proved an overwhelmingly favorable reaction to the sketches, but official charges of "psychological unfitness" prevailed, and the project was abandoned. A painful loss of time, work— and enthusiasm. But Shahn's sketches for the narrow and difficult prison corridor had taught him a control of asymmetric contrasts of space and form which he has since utilized to the full.

His first completed mural was the single-wall fresco at Roosevelt, New Jersey (plate 6), a considerable achievement despite its stylistic and ideological debt to Rivera. The fresco is installed in the community center of Jersey Homesteads, a Federal housing development for garment workers where Shahn himself lives. Its statement is the most impassioned the artist has made in a large-scale work, its political message the most explicit. At the left of the wall, immigrants follow Einstein down a gangplank, away from Jew-baiting Germany, past the coffins of the American martyrs, Sacco and Vanzetti. Arrived in this country, the refugees find the contrasts of reality; they sew by hand in poor light, or by machine in good; they sleep in a park or live in a decent home; they work under improved factory conditions or press clothes with heavy irons in a barren, brick stockade. In the fresco's central panel they discover through organized labor the means to guarantee the reforms that appear in the mural's right section: adequate schooling; co-

operative stores; the kind of community planning and building exemplified by Jersey Homesteads itself.

The composition is based on the undulant principle which Shahn had adopted in his Riker's Island sketches; frontal groups of figures are projected against deep boxes of space; architectural diagonals act as splints to lively interplays of human action; the forms zigzag in and out, swelling and receding. The result is an emphasis on dramatic contrasts of identity and scale, here perhaps too closely knit and dependent on Rivera. The emphasis has been retained in much of Shahn's subsequent easel and mural painting; he habitually creates a psychological as well as a schematic tension between the segments of his compositions. "(But) most important," he said recently, "is always to have a play back and forth, back and forth. Between the big and the little, the light and the dark, the smiling and the sad, the serious and the comic. I like to have three vanishing points in one plane, or a half dozen in three planes."

In 1938 Shahn and his wife, Bernarda Bryson, began work on thirteen fresco panels for the lobby of the Bronx post office in New York; the task was completed in August, 1939. Since the building is used by a large and changing urban population, rather than by members of a small community of professionally related workers, Shahn decided to create a geographic panorama from which visitors might learn something of their vast nation—the South and the North, agriculture and industry, city and country, planner and worker, and presiding over all, Walt Whitman as teacher and prophet.

Shahn had traveled widely in America during his years with the Farm Security Administration, and he now drew on a stored imagery of the various regions, sometimes in the form of photographs he had taken. In place of the divisional symbolism of the Jersey Homesteads wall, he substituted a more spontaneous and monumental iconography. His figures are still dramatized through distortions of scale and placing, but they are handled with new fluency and conviction, their plasticity strengthened by fuller use of color in modeling (plate 8b). Though Shahn himself typically prefers the Jersey Homesteads mural because of its intimate identification with its audience, the Bronx

panels are a far more impressive esthetic achievement. Observe, for example, the soft, devotional concentration of the Negro who gathers cotton as if it were manna (plate 8a), the skill and inventiveness of *Textile Mills* (plate 10), with its masterly definition of perspective and clean grasp of inanimate forms. Yet even more exceptional than Shahn's technical prowess is the emotional warmth of the Bronx murals as a whole. In an era when fresco painting has often assumed machinery's cold dryness, Shahn retains an almost romantic intensity of mood. In the Bronx panels he transcends Rivera's schooling to make his own statement, in which may be felt an open and fervid love of the American people and land.

Shahn continued meanwhile to paint easel pictures. The economic distress of the mid-1930's is reflected in certain of his paintings of this period, their anger and protest aroused by incidents he witnessed on his travels through the country. But when he exhibited his easel pictures in 1940, he was revealed not only as a powerful satirist still, but as one of the most gracious of modern American artists. From a savage commentary on a West Virginia coal

11

strike (plate 9) he could turn to the poignant *Vacant Lot* (plate 16), so penetrating in its evocation of childhood isolation and absorption in play. Soon afterwards he produced the rapt image of a solitary workman playing "Pretty Girl Milking the Cow" to the flutter of autumn leaves (plate 13). Henceforth his easel subjects are often presented as if viewed through one end of a telescope or the other. His figures loom large and near, or are dwarfed by an intervening space which emphasizes their emotional segregation, their peculiarly American loneliness.

In paintings belonging to both categories, Shahn has restated the esthetic of "unbalance and surprise" which Degas had founded out of a dual regard for the casual, shocking patterns of Japanese prints and of instantaneous photographs. This esthetic had affected certain American painters of the 1880's and 1890's, not only the celebrated expatriates, Whistler and Mary Cassatt, but also William M. Chase in *Hide and Seek* and Thomas W. Dewing almost continuously, and it has been a conscious influence for older living artists, notably Edward Hopper. But Shahn goes beyond his predecessors in his seizure of the split-second juxta-

positions furnished by accident, as though his eye's shutter were capable of faster speeds. His approach to photography was almost certainly dictated by his vision as a painter. Nevertheless, it is significant that as a photographer he has often used the device known as the right-angle view finder, as may be seen in one of his self-portraits (plate 20). The device makes formal composition difficult, but encourages spontaneity by permitting the photographer to record his subjects unawares. And while Shahn's acute sense of dramatic off-balance has perhaps been sharpened by his own experience with a camera, it owes something to the photographs of Walker Evans and even more to the superb snapshots of Henri Cartier-Bresson, exhibited in New York in 1933, which revealed the extraordinary tensions underlying commonplace actions if "stopped" by a super-sensitive eye.

It remains to be said that while Shahn's painting often records a photographically arrested reality, its impact is quickened by the most exacting and imaginative painterly means. For example, he originally photographed the scene which appears in *Handball* (plate 15). The painting retains the photograph's opposition of small, dark figures to bright, looming wall; its young athletes are realistic in type and stance. But the painting's architectural background is a composite of New York buildings, and the figures are reduced in number and drastically rearranged by comparison with the photograph. Even when Shahn works quite directly from a photograph, as in *The Welders* (plate 25), he produces a separate image, in this case through a structural aggrandizement which recalls certain figures in Piero della Francesca's Arezzo frescoes in hushed clarity and monumentality. In brief, Shahn uses photography as other artists use preliminary sketches, and from its notations proceeds under the compulsion of a painter's inner vision.

From 1940 to 1942 Shahn executed murals for the Social Security Building in Washington, D.C.: three large rectangular panels, faced by a continuous fresco wall broken by three doorways. The latter wall shows the Family in the center, flanked on the right by Home Building and Food, on the left by Employment through Public Works and by Education and Recreation for Children. The panels opposite refer to those whom Social Security may most benefit—the old, the crippled, the Negro, the young and poor, migratory workers. Both walls include enlargements of earlier easel works. The school boys playing basketball are projected against *Handball's* composition (plates 14, 15); the lone figure of *Vacant Lot* appears twice; a central group is based on the painting, *Willis Avenue Bridge* (plate 11). The change of scale from easel work to mural motif is persuasively effected, though a special virtue of Shahn's easel art is its tight condensation. The Washington murals are far brighter in color than those in the Bronx; the areas are more open; the action more continuously frontal; the contrasts of form less extreme. The result is a new serenity and decorative cohesion which leaves behind both the strenuous didactics of Shahn's Jersey Homesteads wall and the atmospheric romanticism of his Bronx panels.

However impressive Shahn may be as a muralist, he is first and foremost an easel painter. He began his career by creating closely related works in series. He has developed over the past six years into one of the most varied of living American painters, not only as to pictorial discovery but in prevailing mood and expressive means. In an age when a discouraging number of artists have passed in youth the climax of their creative powers, Shahn has grown steadily more eloquent and assured.

In the beginning he depended primarily on line for both structure and accent. His drawing remains the backbone of his art, and perhaps nowhere can his gifts for plastic organization be seen more clearly than in the drawing here reproduced (plate 18). If we compare this drawing with the painting for which it is a study (plate 19), we can understand how sure and strong is his instinct for abstract design, how inspired his feeling for emotional counterpoint. The two figures in the drawing are separated by mostly blank paper, yet they are as tautly related as in the painting itself; the heart-shaped girl skipping rope is as evocatively placed against jagged contours of broken wall. The pose of the figures in the painting seems "accidental." It is revealed in the drawing as the result of brilliant formal invention as well.

In recent years Shahn has used linear and tonal modeling with equal authority, as may be seen in *Hunger* (plate 32), where the chiaroscuro of the head is complemented by the bold contours defining the hand. He has learned lately to apply transparent over opaque tones, with resultant increase in luminosity and textural vivacity. His color itself has become more and more sensitive, and whereas in earlier paintings he often worked within a close tonal range, now his palette is changeable and rich. In many recent works a blood red recurs with symbolic persistence, as in the felled trees of certain landscape passages or the steps ascending the ruins in *The Red Stairway* (plate 23).

A glance through the later plates in this book will reveal Shahn's freshness of imagination: we need only compare *Portrait of Myself When Young* with *Reconstruction*, or *Liberation* with *Hunger*, to appreciate his capacity for renewal (plates 21, 28, 29, 32). He can be ferociously witty, as in the *Self Portrait Among the Churchgoers* (plate 20), which takes revenge for a sermon preached in the Bronx against his murals there. He can be gentle and tender, as in the *Girl Jumping Rope*. He has no fear of sentimentality, knowing that he can give it adequate dignity. He narrows cosmic horror to a dramatic fragment, as in *Pacific Landscape* (plate 30), the climax of a recent perseveration

14

concerned with myriad pebbles. And then abruptly he expands a lyric vision to include the paraphernalia of dreams (plate 27).

There is, however, a constant to be observed in Shahn's painting since roughly 1943. He has become in these recent years more consistently poetic than before, and has shown a formal grace which made itself felt only indirectly in many of his earlier works. The war appears to have released his compassion in more elegiac terms. Though no image of battle could be more grim than *Death on the Beach* (plate 31), for the most part his reaction to world devastation has been expressed as lyric mourning. He has dwelt particularly on architecture in ruins, and his sorrow has attached to Italy, where almost no fallen stone has merely common meaning. Yet it is as though a relentless faith has relieved the horror he felt at war. Children rather than warriors are his usual protagonists, and he has often projected their inextinguishable imaginative life against scenes of desolation. In *Reconstruction*, Italian children pose and teeter upon the shattered blocks of ancient civilization.

Has Shahn's sympathy for the people of Europe led him nearer European sources of art? At any rate, his recent painting, if still plainly American, is linked as never before to those foreign artists, from the fourteenth century Sienese through Fra Angelico to the seventeenth century brothers Le Nain, whose vision was distinguished by a kind of elegant humility. He has progressed lately to a closer communion with lyric, world tradition, though he has sacrificed none of his originality or vigor. The idyllic figure carrying a basket in *The Red Stairway* contrasts startlingly with the 1932 image of Governor Rolph. The pole in *Liberation* is as bright and enchanted as a maypole by Ambrogio Lorenzetti; the child at the left of the composition is like an early Renaissance angel of Annunciation—a very far cry indeed from the stumpy figure in *Sunday Painting* (plate 12). Yet Shahn's recent pictures still derive their vitality from the humanism and love of truth which engendered his first mature works. He painted *Liberation* only after he had seen children swinging wildly in his yard, half in pleasure and half in pop-eyed fear, when it was announced that France was free. The children's legs are piercingly real in weight and flourish. The picture's architectural rubble was painted from a handful of gravel brought in from Shahn's driveway.

"You cannot invent the shape of a stone," the artist explains. But Shahn, who respects reality's humblest fragment, belongs to the rare company of those painters who have achieved a totally creative ambiance for facts. He is becoming known abroad as an artist whose contribution is internationally valid. In this country we can say pridefully that our Federal Government has given him four mural commissions, that our State Department has bought two of his paintings, that our museums own a dozen of his finest works. After an early career studded with rebuffs, he has emerged as one of the most successful of our living painters Therein lies a paradox. For Shahn, who belongs to the Left, is appreciated by both Left and Right; his work has been published in conservative magazines as often as in liberal; he has fulfilled commissions for labor unions and for industrial corporations; his paintings are bought on completion by collectors of every political hue.

A paradoxical situation, yes—but one of immense reassurance for American artists and plain citizens alike. No one has told Shahn what or how to paint. He has worked from personal conviction, under no imposed directive or compulsion. So doing, he has earned an acclaim which, though in no sense popular as yet, is in diversity something of a tribute to this country's critical resilience, its willingness to treasure the artist who speaks with sincere authority, in whatever idiom he alone prefers.

James Thrall Soby

PLATES

1: *The Blind Accordion Player*, 1945 (25½ x 38¼, Tempera) Owner, Mr and Mrs Roy R. Neuberger.

2: Sacco-Vanzetti series, *The Lowell Committee*, 1931-32 (11 x 15, Gouache) Private Collection.

3: Sacco-Vanzetti series, *Bartolomeo Vanzetti and Nicola Sacco*, 1931-32 (10½ x 14¼, Gouache) Owner, Museum of Modern Art, New York, gift of Mrs John D. Rockefeller, Jr.

4: Mooney series, (*a*) *Gov. James Rolph Jr of California*, 1932 (16½ x 12, Gouache) Owner S. J. Perelman. (*b*) *My Son is Innocent*, 1932 (14 x 11, Gouache) Owner, Edward B. Rowan.

5: Mooney series, *Two Witnesses, Mellie and Sadie Edeau*, 1932 (12 x 16, Gouache) Owner, Museum of Modern Art, New York.

6: Fresco Mural in the Community Center at Jersey Homesteads, Roosevelt, New Jersey, 1938-39. Commissioned by Farm Security Administration.

7: Prohibition series, *W.C.T.U. Parade*, 1933-34 (16 x 31⅓, Gouache) Owner, Public Works of Art Project, courtesy Museum of the City of New York.

8: (*a*) *Picking Cotton*, 1938-39, (*b*) *Baling Cotton*, 1938-39. Fresco Mural in United States Government Post Office, Bronx Central Annex, New York. Commissioned by Section of Fine Arts, Public Buildings Administration, United States Treasury.

9: *Scott's Run, West Virginia*, 1937 (22½ x 28, Gouache) Owner, Whitney Museum of American Art.

10: *Textile Mills*, 1938-39. Detail of Murals in United States Government Post Office, Bronx Central Annex, New York.

11: *Willis Avenue Bridge*, 1940 (22¼ x 30½, Tempera) Owner, Lincoln Kirstein.

12: *Sunday Painting*, 1938 (16⅛ x 24, Tempera) Owner, Mrs Ben Shahn.

13: *Pretty Girl Milking The Cow*, 1940 (22 x 30, Tempera) Private Collection.

14: Detail of Fresco Mural in Social Security Building, Washington, D.C., 1940-42. Commissioned by Section of Fine Arts, Public Buildings Administration, United States Treasury.

PLATES

15: *Handball*, 1939 (22¾ x 31¼, Tempera)
Owner, Museum of Modern Art, New York, Mrs John D. Rockefeller, Jr., Purchase Fund.

16: *Vacant Lot*, 1939 (19 x 23, Tempera) Owner, Wadsworth Atheneum, Hartford, Connecticut.

17: *Peter and The Wolf*, 1943 (6 x 9, Tempera) Owner, Mr and Mrs Joseph Louchheim.

18: *Girl Jumping Rope*, 1943 (22 x 30, Ink) Private Collection.

19: *Girl Jumping Rope*, 1943 (19¾ x 27½, Tempera) Owner, Richard Loeb.

20: *Self Portrait Among The Churchgoers*, 1939 (20 x 29, Tempera) Owner, Richard Loeb.

21: *Portrait of Myself When Young*, 1943 (19¾ x 27½, Tempera) Owner, Miss Celia Hubbard.

22: *Four Piece Orchestra*, 1944 (18 x 24, Tempera) Owner, S. J. Perelman.

23: *The Red Stairway*, 1944 (16 x 23½, Tempera) Owner, City Art Museum of St. Louis.

24: *Inflation Means Hunger. Register, Vote.* Poster for the Political Action Committee, C.I.O., 1946 (41 x 28)
Owner, Museum of Modern Art, New York.

25: *The Welders*, 1944 (22 x 39¾, Tempera) Owner, Museum of Modern Art, New York.

26: *Carnival*, 1946 (22 x 30, Tempera) Owner, Mr and Mrs Benjamin Tepper.

27: *Cherubs and Children*, 1944 (15½ x 23½, Tempera) Owner, Whitney Museum of American Art.

28: *Reconstruction*, 1945 (26 x 39, Tempera) Owner, Whitney Museum of American Art.

29: *Liberation*, 1945 (30 x 39½, Tempera) Private Collection.

30: *Pacific Landscape*, 1945 (25½ x 39, Tempera) Owner, Downtown Gallery, New York.

31: *Death on the Beach*, 1945 (10 x 14, Tempera) Owner, Mr and Mrs Sidney Berkowitz.

32: *Hunger*, 1946 (40 x 26, Tempera) Owner, United States Department of State.

Plate 1 *The Blind Accordion Player* 1945

Plate 2 *The Lowell Committee* 1931–32

Plate 3 *Bartolomeo Vanzetti and Nicola Sacco* 1931–32

Plate 4 (a) *Governor James Rolph Jr of California* 1932
(b) *My Son is Innocent* 1932

Plate 5 *Two Witnesses, Mellie Edeau and Sadie Edeau* 1932

Plate 6 *Fresco Mural* 1938-39

Plate 7 *W.C.T.U. Parade* 1933–34

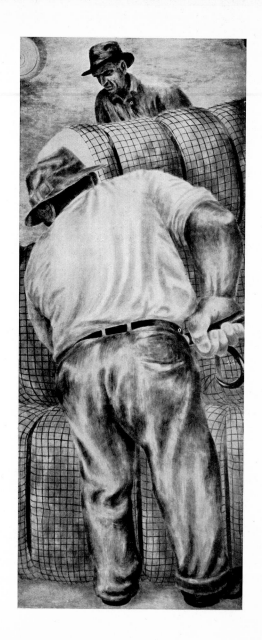

Plate 8 (a) *Picking Cotton* 1938–39
(b) *Baling Cotton* 1938–39

Plate 9 *Scott's Run, West Virginia* 1937

Plate 10 *Textile Mills* 1938–39

Plate 11 *Willis Avenue Bridge* 1940

Plate 12 *Sunday Painting* 1938

Plate 13 *Pretty Girl Milking The Cow* 1940

Plate 14 *Detail of Fresco Mural* 1940–42

Plate 15 *Handball* 1939

Plate 16 *Vacant Lot* 1939

Plate 17 *Peter And The Wolf* 1943

Plate 18 *Girl Jumping Rope* 1943

Plate 19 *Girl Jumping Rope* 1943

Plate 20 *Self Portrait Among The Churchgoers* 1939

Plate 21 *Portrait of Myself When Young* 1943

Plate 22 *Four Piece Orchestra* 1944

Plate 23 *The Red Stairway* 1944

Plate 24 *Inflation Means Hunger. Register, Vote* 1946

Plate 25 *The Welders* 1944

Plate 26 *Carnival* 1946

Plate 27 *Cherubs and Children* 1944

Plate 28 *Reconstruction* 1945

Plate 29 *Liberation* 1945

Plate 30 *Pacific Landscape* 1945

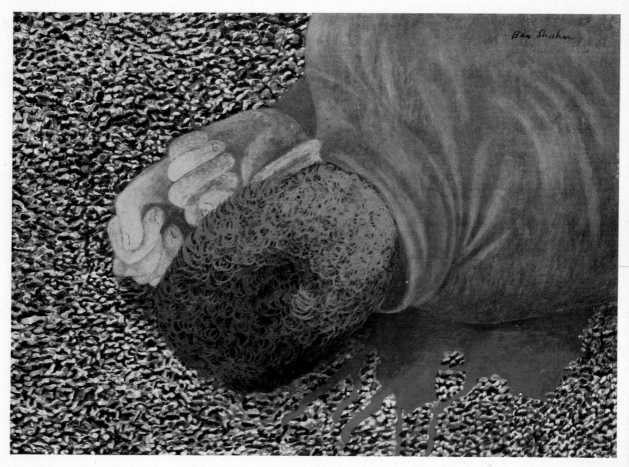

Plate 31 *Death On The Beach* 1945

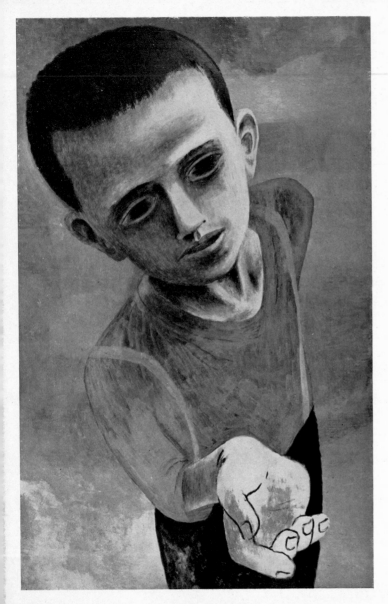

Plate 32 *Hunger* 1946